# The Vulture and the Queen

The Battle of the Billionaire and the Botox Queen

## Hoyt Hilsman

# INTRODUCTION

It's a mid-July day at the Estadio do Maracana in Rio de Janeiro. Argentina and Germany are battling it out in the finals of the 2014 FIFA World Cup. At the end of regulation time, the score is tied at 0-0. With the whole world watching and the fans from both countries praying for a victory, German attacker Andre Schurrle, a late game substitute, drives past three Argentine defenders, passing to 22-year old Mario Gotze, who deftly cushions the ball off his chest and then kicks it past goalkeeper Sergio Romero for the winning goal. The stadium erupts in hysteria as the German fans go wild. Immediate celebrations begin in every corner of Germany, while Argentinians sit in stunned silence, some weeping quietly.

Among the fans in the Estadio do Maracana rooting for Argentina this day is a gray-haired American in his late-sixties, wearing glasses and an Argentine team jersey. The man looks like a college professor who has spent a lifetime in some ivory tower, perhaps studying obscure medieval texts, but nothing could be further from the truth. He is Paul Singer, founder of a powerful hedge fund, a billionaire many times over. What's more, as he cheers for Argentina, he holds the future of forty million Argentinians in his hands.

At the same time, sitting in the Presidential box high above the crowd are Dilma Rousseff, the President of Brazil, and Angela Merkel, the Chancellor of Germany. Noticeably absent at this historic moment in her nation's history is Cristina Fernandez de Kirchner, the President of Argentina. Why, wondered many Argentines, would "Queen Cristina," as she has been called, fail to attend their country's greatest sporting event in a quarter of a century?

Earlier in the week, Kirchner's office had released a statement that she would not attend the World Cup final because of a throat infection. Why then would she schedule a meeting the day before the final with Russian President Vladimir Putin? And why would she continue with her plans to attend a summit of emerging powers the following week in Brazil?

Kirchner also mentioned in the statement that she was going to attend her grandson's first birthday the day after the World Cup final. "As a grandmother, you can imagine how eager I am to share this event with my family," said Kirchner. But many of her fellow citizens – seized by soccer mania and the joy over Argentina reaching the World Cup – were not buying it. Was it a slap in the face of the country's macho soccer culture? Or was she afraid that Argentina will lose and she will be accused on jinxing them by her presence? "Presidents in the past have been stigmatized for not bringing national teams any luck," wrote the *Buenos Aires Herald*, "Tiny a thought as it may sound, Cristina

Fernández might not want to expose herself to a defeat at a time her administration is facing a hardship or two. Nobody wants to be the next jinx."

For Argentina – and many other countries around the world – soccer is akin to a national religion. The soccer team is synonymous with the nation. The two are inseparable and national identity is inextricable woven into the fate of the team. When it comes to great events like a World Cup final, there is no distinction between sports and politics. So in the tangled politics of Argentina, Kirchner's decision to miss the final was a reflection of her precarious status. The nickname "Queen Cristina," once been a proud emblem of her popularity, was now muttered – and often shouted – on the streets of Argentina as a mark of derision. .

What led to the downfall of Cristina Kirchner from her historic role as the first female President of Argentina -- and a widely popular figure -- to a roundly criticized and scorned politician? What was behind the decline of Argentina from a booming economy to a nation facing bankruptcy? And what was the role of the graying, professorial man sitting in the stands at the Estadio do Maracana? This book will explore that fascinating story.

# CHAPTER ONE

The celebration of her grandson's first birthday in her home town of Patagonian town of Río Gallegos was a rare moment of joy for Cristina Fernandez de Kirchner. The past few years had been difficult ones for the first democratically elected female President of Argentina. In 2007, she had won a decisive victory in the presidential election, succeeding her husband Nestor Kirchner and avoiding a runoff by capturing more than 45% of the vote, mostly from poor and working class voters. Since then, they had faced crisis after crisis, and a slow decline in popularity. But together, the Kirchners had soldiered through troubled times.

From the time they met as university students and activists in the leftist Personist cause, Nestor Kirchner and Cristina Fernandez were a dynamic political and romantic partnership. It was an instant love match between the charismatic and forceful Nestor and the determined and steely Cristina. Both came from modest working class backgrounds -- Cristina's father was a bus driver and Nestor's was a postal official. Both were ambitious and deeply committed to leftist politics. They had met at a leftist student rally, quickly became a couple and were married six months later. Soon after their marriage, Cristina switched her studies from psychology to law. After getting her law degree, she joined her husband in his private legal practice.

Both Kirchners had been born at a time when Argentina was deeply divided over the presidency of Juan Peron, and later that of his wife, the famous Evita. The Perons and their leftist followers, the Peronists, were widely loved by Argentina's poor and working class, but despised by most of the middle and upper classes, as well as elements of the military. Cristina grew up in the midst of this turbulent era in the city of La Plata, which had been briefly renamed for Eva Peron until one of the many military dictatorships changed it back to its original name. Cristina's family was a reflection of the political divisions in the country. Her father was a strong anti-Peronist, while her mother, a trade union leader of German descent, was an equally strong Peronist. The family environment was understandably tense, and Cristina's parents, who had not even married until she was two years old, eventually divorced.

After the military coup in 1976 against President Isabel Peron, the third wife and widow of Juan Peron, the dictatorship launched the "dirty war" against Peronists, journalists, trade unionists and other leftists. The Kirchners had been deeply involved in left-wing politics, beginning as students when Nestor had been present at the infamous Ezeiza airport massacre at which right-wing snipers killed or injured hundreds of Peronists who were greeting Juan Peron upon his return to Argentina after an eighteen-year exile. In earlier years, the Kirchners had even made a few contacts with leftist guerillas, but they managed to avoid serious scrutiny (although Cristina spent a month in jail before being freed).

Because of their leftist sympathies, they decided to keep a low profile during the time, moving to remote Patagonia where they set up a legal practice. However, when democracy was restored in 1983, both Kirchners re-entered politics. By 1987, Nestor was elected mayor of the city of Rio Gallegos and in 1991 was elected governor of the province of Santa Cruz. In the meantime, Cristina had given birth to their son Maximo and had been elected to the provincial legislature of Santa Cruz.

Nestor consolidated his power in Santa Cruz, amending the provincial constitution to allow him to run for re-election indefinitely. Soon he was a rising star in the Judicialist (Peronist) party, which was led by President Carlos Menem. An intraparty dispute arose in 1999 when Menem sought to run for a third, unconstitutional term as President. Nestor supported Menem's opponent Eduardo Duhalde, who was defeated in his run for the presidency. In the meantime, Cristina had been elected to the National Chamber of Deputies in 1995 and the Senate in 2001.

2003 was a pivotal year in the life of the Kirchners. Argentina was enduring a deep economic crisis, which included a run on the banks and riots in the streets. A series of interim presidents and street demonstrations ended with a strong public rejection of the entire political class – the Argentinian equivalent of "throw the bums out!" Into this morass stepped Nestor Kirchner in the 2003 presidential election. In a crowded field, including former president Menem, Nestor came in second with 22% of the vote. In the runoff election, Menem withdrew and Kirchner was declared president in May, 2003, elected with the lowest voting percentage in Argentina's history.

Immediately upon assuming office, Nestor took an aggressive approach toward the economic crisis and the human suffering that it had caused. He also attacked corruption in the government, forcibly retiring military leaders and Supreme Court justices. But his most controversial and important contribution was dealing with Argentina's $178 billion debt. In tough negotiations with the International Monetary Fund, Nestor was able to renegotiate more than three-quarters of the national debt for a recovery value of about one-third of its original value. By 2005, he was able to announce the full repayment of Argentina's debt.

When Nestor took office, Argentina had defaulted on its debt, its GDP had declined by nearly 20% in four years, unemployment reached 25%, and the peso had depreciated 70%. From 2003 until 2007, the economy grew 9% annually with nearly 5 million jobs added. By the end of his first term, Nestor was hugely popular and expected to win a second term easily -- until he decided not to run. It is still something of a mystery as why Nestor decided not to run for a second term, especially since he was riding a wave of popularity. There had been some whispers of corruption, but that rarely would drive a South American leader out of office. A more plausible explanation is a political one – he wanted to extend his power for a longer period by turning the reins over to Cristina. Since a president is limited to two terms in office, why not let Cristina take over (she would be sure to win in 2007 on his coattails) and remain the power behind the throne? That way, she could serve two terms and he could return, if necessary, for an additional term. In short, the Kirchners hoped to build a dynasty.

Whatever the reason for Nestor's retirement, he campaigned heavily for Cristina and she won a decisive victory in 2007, avoiding a runoff by capturing more than 45% of the vote, mostly from poor and working class voters. Riding on a wave of popularity, Cristina launched an aggressive campaign against the entrenched agricultural interests, which represented one of the most elite groups in the country. She raised taxes on agricultural exports, which led to boycotts and protests by the agricultural sectors, and the effort was defeated and Cristina's approval rating plummeted.

Over the next several years, Cristina struggled to maintain her popularity, even as her political power was diminished by a loss of seats in the Congress and by allegations of impropriety that plagued her administration. At the same time, her international stature grew as she championed Argentina's interests by visits to numerous countries and global and regional summits. She also worked to improve the economy and reduce Argentina's debt, and she was outspoken in her continued fight with Britain to regain control of the Falkland Islands.

However, allegations of impropriety contributed increasingly to the Kirchners' decline in approval, including charges of corruption. Their wealth had grew by seven times since Nestor's election in 2003, in part the result of questionable land deals in their home town of El Calafate. Cristina was also criticized for her extravagant lifestyle, which included shopping sprees and cosmetic surgery (although Cristina denies ever going under the knife).

Always by her side and working tirelessly behind the scenes was Nestor, whom many Argentinians believed was the power behind the throne. Whatever the reality was, Cristina and Nestor were seen as a dynamic power couple who had restored some of Argentina's former glory, whatever the current difficulties. They were known around the world as Latin America's "power couple" in the mold of Bill and Hillary Clinton. However, all that was to come crashing down in the fall of 2010 as tragedy suddenly descended on their family and the nation.

CHAPTER TWO

Paul Singer grew up worlds away from Cristina and Nestor Kirchner, but their paths would cross in ways that threatened to send Argentina into financial freefall. Singer was born in 1944 and grew up in the comfortable suburb of Tenafly, New Jersey. One of three children, his father was a pharmacist who commuted to Manhattan and his mother was a homemaker. The young Paul showed early talent as a musician, and studied classical music from the age of ten, until rock and roll seized his imagination, and he became a fan of Led Zeppelin and other rock groups.

Singer majored in psychology at the University of Rochester, and then graduated from Harvard Law School. He spent a few years with a corporate law firm and then landed a job that would set his life in a new direction. He joined the investment bank of Donaldson, Lufkin and Jenrette. Founded in 1959 as a Wall Street Research firm, DLJ had become the hottest outfit on the Street in the 1970's and go-go '80's. The expanded from research into the rapidly growing field of investment banking and private equity, acquiring Drexel Burnham Lambert's high-yield bond team when that company failed, and growing large merchant banking, investment and real estate operations.

Many of the mega-stars of investment banking, private equity and the hedge fund world, not to mention leading figures in the public sector, came out of the DLJ shops during the boom years of Wall Street. Singer clearly learned a lot while he was at DLJ, including the lesson that you could make a great deal more money starting your own firm than spending your life working in the DLJ sweatshop. So, like a lot of DLJ, alumni, the thirty-three year old Singer struck out on his own, launching Elliott Associates in 1977 with $1.3 million from family and friends.

Things did not go well for Singer in the early years of Elliott Associates. He sustained heavy stock losses, which left him with an aversion to risk that still guides his investment strategy. A CNN profile of Singer notes that "he rarely uses leverage to juice returns." Early on, Singer began focusing on distressed assets – buying up the debt of bankrupt companies and forcing repayment through the courts or by other strong-arming, albeit legal. This tactic has earned his fund the moniker of "vulture fund," but has brought it a strong record of success. Since the founding of Elliott in the late '70's, the firm has averaged 14% annual returns, significantly more than the S&P 500 index. Singer's fund has been involved in lots of post-collapse corporate restructurings, including Chrysler and auto parts supplier Delphi. But he is best known for snapping up sovercign debt.

Sovereign debt is basically bonds or other debt that a nation issues to finance itself. The risk of sovereign debt depends on the stability of the government, whether it is a developed or developing nation, the credit rating of the government and the state of its currency. Throughout modern history, there have been a number of countries that have defaulted on their debts. Until the 1950's, most nations enjoyed sovereign immunity from debt collection. The doctrine was modified in the 1950's when nations became liable for their debt.

Most of the time, however, the international banking system has taken a fairly forgiving approach to sovereign debt defaults. With the help of the International Monetary Fund, most nations have been able to "restructure" their debts, often paying off a fraction of the debt to their creditors. This traditional approach was seen as important to preserving the stability of the international monetary system, and providing some protection for weaker nations. The creditors – mostly large banking institutions – were willing to go along with the restructuring to preserve stability in the system, and were often happy to get repayment of a least part of the debt. Until Paul Singer came along.

Beginning in the mid-'90's, Singer began buying sovereign debt from creditors at a discount on the chance that he could force the debtor nation to pay all or at least a significant portion of the debt. His strategy was to collect the money through the U.S. court system and then enforce the judgment against the debtor country. In 1996 he purchased defaulted Peruvian debt for a reported $11.4 million – a fraction of its face value – and then he sued Peru in a U.S. court. The court ruled against Singer under a New York law that followed the common law doctrine of "champerty," derived from a medieval English law which forbade the purchasing of a debt for the sole purpose of suing the debtor.

However, the Peru ruling was overturned on appeal in 2000 when Singer was awarded a $58 million judgment. It was one of the most important cases in the area of sovereign debt and opened the door for the purchase – and more importantly the collection – of foreign debt. As a practical matter, Singer still had several hurdles to actually collecting the debt from the various banks and agents of Peru, but he fought in both U.S. and foreign courts, and eventually forced Peru to pay the debt.

As Singer and Elliott Associates began buying up more sovereign debt, they became known as the pre-eminent "vulture fund" – picking at the carcasses of debtor nations and forcing them through the legal system to make good on their debts, even when it meant that the people of the debtor country would suffer. Singer's critics have argued over the years that his strategy, while technically legal, is immoral. He has been called the "inventor of vulture funds," and has been roundly criticized in international circles for taking money from poor nations that could be going to schools, roads, health care and reduction of poverty. Singer has answered his critics by arguing that his fund is simply a bondholder seeking to collect legal debts.

While Singer and his Elliott Associates had managed to keep a low profile for a long time, it was not just his relentless pursuit of sovereign debt, but also his political activism that has raised his profile significantly. Over the past few years, Singer has emerged as a quiet but powerful force in the Republican party. He was perhaps the most important "bundler" – commanding a large network of rich donors – for the Romney campaign in 2012. He also has given nearly $2 million in recent years to Republicans in local races in Florida, Michigan, California and Texas.

But it's not only his prodigious fundraising that gives Paul Singer his clout. He is also something of an intellectual leader for the elite wing of the donor class, working tenaciously to roll back government regulation and oppose higher taxes on the wealthy. In letters to investors, he has warned of "mass poverty and degradation of freedom" unless America abandons its current course. He is a regular speaker at financial industry functions and is chair of a conservative think tank that is extreme but his right-wing views. Singer breaks ranks with most conservatives with his support of gay rights. He has given over $8 million to nonprofits supporting gay rights, and helped to bankroll the

New York same-sex initiative. One of his sons, Andrew. is gay and was married in Massachusetts.

Singer has engaged in a long-running battle with government agencies and regulators. He opposes the Dodd-Frank banking regulations, arguing that they "enshrine" too-big-to-fail banks. He plays hardball in courtrooms and with government and industry regulators. When the Financial Industry Regulatory Authority worked to resolve claims in the Lehman Brothers bankruptcy case, Singer and Elliott Associates, which had bought a significant amount of Lehman debt for as little as 9 cents on the dollar, were unyielding in their demands. The lead attorney for Lehman, Harvey Miller, said of Elliott "They are very hard-nosed, very aggressive and sometimes inflexible. They just take a position and say 'That's the way it has to be because we say so.'" Elliott came away from the Lehman settlement with a substantial profit.

Singer and Elliott insist that they only go after "bad actors." But it is clear that the fund picks its targets carefully, selecting only those with an ability to pay. Elliott Management bought $32.6 million in loan debt of the Republic of Congo, reportedly for less than $2.3 million. It sued in a British court and was awarded more than $100 million, including penalties and interest. As part of its campaign to collect the debt, Elliott exposed widespread corruption by the government of the Congo. The government eventually settled for an estimated $90 million. Observers from the IMF to former Treasury Secretary Hank Paulson have roundly criticized the practice of extracting large profits from poor countries in default.

For thirty-five years, Paul Singer and Elliott Associates have been riding high on the profits from their strategy of buying up "distressed assets" and then aggressively pursuing payment from debtor countries and nations. Singer scoffs at the label of "vulture fund," but has been increasingly vilified for the practice. As he returned from the World Cup final in July, 2014, he commanded considerable power both in financial and political circles. But he was facing a showdown in less than three weeks in a federal court in New York. He had picked a fight with a formidable adversary -- "Queen Cristina" of Argentina – and it was anybody's guess as to who would come out on top.

CHAPTER THREE

In late October, 2010, Nestor and Cristina Kirchner were enjoying a respite from the pressures of the presidency at their home in the town of El Calafate in the remote Patagonian region. El Calafate had been the couple's retreat ever since they escaped the ravages of Argentina's "Dirty War" against leftists in the '70's and '80's. Earlier in the year, Nestor had suffered health problems and had undergone bypass surgery for blocked arteries. His doctor had prescribed an extended period of rest, but his strength was now returning, and plans were reportedly being made for Nestor to run for president, replacing Cristina, who had suffered considerably under the pressure of the office.

However, everything changed on the evening of October 26th, when Nestor began complaining of flu-like symptoms. He condition worsened in the early morning hours of October 27th when he lost consciousness and was rushed to a nearby hospital. At 9:15 a.m. Nestor Kirchner was pronounced dead. The cause of death – cardiac arrest. Nothing had prepared the Kirchner family or the Argentine nation for Nestor's sudden death. Despite his heart problems, there was no indication that his life had been in danger.

The outpouring of grief in Argentina was overwhelming. Hundreds of thousands of Argentines walked past Nestor's casket lying in state at Casa Rosada, the presidential palace. His funeral was attended by heads of state from all over Latin America, including Bolivia's Evo Morales, Brazil's Lula da Silva and Venezuela's Hugo Chavez, who was continuously at Cristina's side and attended the private family funeral service. Tens of thousands of mourners crowded the street and politicians from all factions shared in the sudden loss of the man who had rescued Argentina from a serious economic crisis.

For Cristina, the loss of her husband was devastating, both personally and politically. For more than three years after his death, she wore only black in public appearances. While some criticized her motives, suggesting that she was trying to win sympathy from the Argentine public, there is little question that her grief was genuine. She had lost her romantic and political partner, and would struggle mightily to recover. Their presidencies were, for many Argentinians, a symbol not only of a strong political partnership, but also of the power of romantic love in a turbulent world. His sudden death would resonate for years into the future, both for Cristina's presidency and for the fate of the Argentinian nation.

As a political wife and President of the nation, Cristina understood what she had to do. She resumed her public duties, attending the G20 summit in Seoul and resuming talks on the restructuring of Argentina's debts. With the election of 2011 approaching, she began several aggressive initiatives, including a series of highly publicized disagreements with Brazil over trade quotas, as well as the ongoing dispute with Great Britain over Argentina's claim to the Falkland Islands. She declared her candidacy for a second term in June, and was re-elected with 54% of the vote in October.

After winning the election handily and gaining control of both chambers of Congress, Cristina began a program of fiscal reform, which included tax increases and limits on wage hikes, as well as trade protectionism and reorganization of state-owned enterprises. The country's leading labor leader, long a supporter of the Kirchners, began to oppose Cristina and her government's initiatives. A year into her second term, currency controls which led to a rampant black market, as well as a series of political scandals that rocked her government, led to a decline in her popularity. By the end of 2012, thousands of citizens were marching in the street to protest Cristina's rule.

As her popularity plummeted, Cristina's personal style came under renewed criticism. While she had once been heralded as the "new Evita," her glamorous profile now became a liability. In a country where medical tourism for plastic surgery is booming, and where one out of every thirty Argentinians will have cosmetic surgery, Cristina was criticized for her facelifts (which she denies ever having) and her botox treatments, which earned her the nickname of "Botox Queen," not to mention her elegant outfits. In one highly publicized incident in 2011, she reportedly spent $110,000 on 20 pairs of Christian Louboutin shoes in Paris after meeting with President Nicolas Sarkozy. And she was accused of spending $20,000 to have daily newspapers delivered by jet to her vacation home.

More seriously, she faced charges that she and Nestor had profited tremendously by misappropriation of public funds in Patagonia. With many apartments, houses, stores and hotels in their name, the Kirchners wealth was pegged at nearly $20 million, much of it located in their home town of El Calafate, a small town whose primary industry is glacier and wildlife tourism. While more than three thousand local residents had filed to by small lots after the Kirchners had an airport built there in 2000, many of them were denied permits after the Kirchners and other government officials jumped to the head of the line. In a highly-publicized case, the Kirchners bought land for $50,000 and sold it two years later for $2.4 million.

Defenders of Cristina argue that she has been unfairly targeted by the Argentine media, with which she has always had a combative relationship. They contend that she has been made a scapegoat by a macho society, especially because of her defense of same-sex marriage. By early 2013, some her critics were questioning her mental health after she broke down in tears while giving a speech about the Dirty War and those who had "disappeared." Wikileaks even released a 2010 cable from then-Secretary of State Hilary Clinton questioning Cristina's mental health.

Then, in October of 2013, Cristina began to experience weakness and numbness in her arm. After a medical examination, the doctors discovered a small blood clot in her brain that may have been caused by a previous head injury. They operated to remove the blood clot and prescribed thirty days of bed rest. While a complete recovery was expected, the timing of the surgery in the midst of midterm elections was unsettling to Argentina's public and political class. By mid-December, 2013, she had still not made any public appearances and never responded to a series of energy and water crises in the country. For many in Argentina, it appeared that the reign of the Kirchners might be over.

# CHAPTER FOUR

A few weeks after Argentina's heartbreaking loss in the World Cup final, intense negotiations were going on at the Park Avenue office of Daniel Pollack, the mediator appointed by a federal court judge to preside over the last-ditch settlement talks between the government of Argentina and the hedge funds – most prominently Singer's Elliott Associates – who were holding out for a better payday on their investment in billions worth of Argentine's bonds.

The origins of the long-running dispute, which had been going on for more than a decade, began when Singer started to accumulate Argentina's debt during the late '90's. His investment totaled bonds with a face value of $630 million, most of it purchased for pennies on the dollar. After Argentina defaulted on its debt in 2002, Singer refused the government's offer of 30 cents on the dollar to the bondholders, even though most investors had reluctantly agreed. Even when Argentina significantly increased its offer in an effort to settle the remaining debt, Singer would not budge.

For years afterward, Singer pursued Argentina in courts around the world, but without much success. In the United States, the New York Federal Reserve refused to release Argentina's central bank deposits to Singer, and the Treasury Department sided with the Fed.

Singer even went to court in Ghana to try and seize an Argentine naval vessel that was in the port of Tema. The court ordered the ship seized, but it was later released. However, a breakthrough in the long-running dispute came for Singer and his allies when they went to Federal District Court in Manhattan.

The presiding judge was 83-year old Judge Thomas Griesa, who had been appointed to the federal bench by President Nixon in 1972. A graduate of Harvard College and Stanford Law School, he had previously been a partner at a Wall Street law firm. Described as "warm and generous" by his staff, Griesa plays the harpsichord in his spare time and eats the same lunch at his desk every day. Griesa sometimes appears short-tempered in the courtroom, and has occasionally been criticized for not being fully aware of the scope of his rulings. However, when he had presided over the restructuring of Argentina's debts in 2005, then-President Nestor Kirchner had said his country was "deeply satisfied" after an appeals court upheld Griesa's ruling that let the restructuring proceed. So no one expected the bombshell that was about to come out of Judge Griesa's courtroom.

Citing a bit of long-forgotten boilerplate language in the Argentine bond agreements, Judge Griesa relied on the ancient doctrine of *pari passu* which says, in essence, that a borrower has to treat all lenders equally. In other words, a debtor can't pay Peter and not pay Paul. In his ruling, Griesa relied on this doctrine to rule that Argentina could not repay the bondholders who had agreed to a settlement deal and at the same time refuse to pay Singer and the other holdouts. In a single stroke, Griesa was wiping out over a decade of Argentina's efforts to settle its debts, not to mention centuries of legal precedent. Finally, Singer had been given the weapon he needed to collect on his Argentina bonds.

The ruling stirred up an immediate firestorm among legal scholars, the financial community and a host of developing nations who saw a future of bankruptcy and endless poverty. How could they ever settle their debts if their creditors could hold out for full repayment? Was this simply a conspiracy by the United States to condemn the poor nations to a bleak future? The Obama administration responded immediately, calling Judge Griesa's decision "impermissibly broad," arguing that it could seriously undermine America's foreign relations. The IMF and other international organization joined the chorus, saying it could disrupt their mission to reduce the debt burden of developing nations. As Nobel Prize –winning economist Joseph Stiglitz wrote "We've had a lot of bombs being thrown around the world, and this is America throwing a bomb into the global economic system. We don't know how big the explosion will be – and it's not just about Argentina."

Despite the outcry, the appeals court upheld Griesa's ruling and the Supreme Court declined to hear Argentina's appeal. In subsequent hearings after the bombshell ruling, it became apparent that the judge had not been fully aware of the implications or scope of his decision. For example, it was reported that he did not know which set of bonds were covered by the ruling. "I may have very well not covered things that should have been covered," said the judge in open court as he issued a clarification. In any case, his ruling will stand and has it made Griesa an object of scorn not only in Argentina, but in poor nations around the world.

For his part, Singer has kept a low profile in the wake of the decision and claims to be bewildered by all the attention the case has commanded. According to colleagues in the hedge-fund world, Singer sees himself simply as a defender of creditors rights and ultimately the rule of law. In the past, he has argued that his fight will be beneficial for debtor nations. "Imagine how much capital a country like Argentina might attract," he wrote in a 2005 article, "if instead of defaulting seriatim and affecting a pose of anger toward creditors, it borrowed responsibly and honored its obligations."

In a letter to Elliott investors in 2014, Singer blasted the media attention that the case had garnered, "Elliott does not seek such publicity. Obviously, our lives would be easier if the press cared less about this particular position and/or similar positions that attract attention." Arguing that his investment strategy was not for the faint of heart, Singer continued "As we have noted, one of the reasons we continue to see attractive opportunities, even in the current yield-hungry environment, is that complex, labor-intensive situations are not everyone's cup of tea."

Singer also wrote that he doesn't like going to court continuously to collect his debts, calling lawsuits "uncertain, expensive, difficult and time-consuming." But Singer also concedes that the high-profile Argentina case would inevitably attract media attention. "While many journalists and commentators badly misunderstand what Elliott is all about, we understand that this publicity is occasionally the cost of adhering to our philosophy, which is to seek truly uncorrelated positions in which the key determinants of unlocking value are our own creativity and hard work."

Despite Singer's lofty posturing, it was clear that Argentina had no desire to pay what they viewed as blackmail by a "vulture" hedge fund. Judge Griesa had set a deadline of July 30 for resolution of the case. As the deadline neared, with no breakthrough in sight, a new player entered the scene – Argentina's "secret weapon" against default. Glamorous, young and ambitious, he would shortly turn the negotiations into a form of high theater rarely witnessed on the international stage.

# CHAPTER FIVE

In late June of 2014, as settlement negotiations were underway in Manhattan between Argentina and its holdout creditors, Axel Kicillof, the young Argentine Minister of Economy with movie star looks and impressive academic credentials, climbed on a jet to New York, ostensibly to address the UN Group of 77 developing nations. However, there was widespread speculation that the powerful Kicillof would intervene in the negotiations, which had reached a stalemate.

In a few short years, Kicillof has soared from an obscure Marxist professor to arguably the most powerful person in Argentina, even more powerful than the President herself. Observers have called him the "strongest economy minister Argentina has had in a decade, comparing him to Nestor Kirchner at the height of his powers. "He's confrontational, outwardly self-confident and sometimes perceived as being arrogant," wrote Ezequiel Burgo in a biography of Kicillof, "which of course makes him stand out at a time like this."

Kicillof is the son of middle-class parents -- a psychiatrist father who committed suicide when Axel was twenty-two and a mother who is a prominent psychologist. As a student at the University of Buenos Aires, Kicillof was the leader of a leftist student organization, and later became a professor there. His writings interpret the work of Keynes and Adam Smith from a Marxist perspective, and he has argued for greater state control of Argentina's economy in times of financial crisis. He was appointed as a deputy minister in 2012 and directed the nationalization of YPF, the Argentine oil company. Kirchner promoted him to Minister of Economy in November, 2013.

Kicillof is known for his modest lifestyle – driving an old Renault compact, forgoing bodyguards and living a restrained life with his wife, a literature professor, and their two children. But his good looks, flamboyant personality and rock-and-roll image have made him a favorite of celebrity magazines. He is trailed frequently by paparazzi, and is often swarmed in public by both admirers and detractors. Kicillof is also known for his obsession with numbers, requesting spreadsheets and other details from oil companies and other large industrial firms. He has also become something of a globetrotter, traveling around the globe in an effort to settle Argentina's far flung debts. His critics contend that Kicillof is in over his head. According to Hector Zumarraga, a labor rights lawyer, "He's not up to the job. He doesn't understand that it's not enough to know just economic theory, and we're seeing proof of that now."

In a firebrand speech to the UN Group of 77, Kicillof said that Griesa's decision would send Argentina's economy into a tailspin. He said if Argentina complied with the ruling it would quickly result in lawsuits from other bondholder who were not part of the original settlement, adding another $15 billion to the country's debt payments. Eventually, creditors who had joined the swap could also sue to demand at least $120 billion in payments on the same terms. For the developing nations, the message was clear. They would all be subject to the reach of the vulture funds if the decision were allowed to stand, and they resolved to protest the judge's ruling.

The speculation in the media and the financial world was that, after giving his speech at the UN, Kicillof would join the settlement talks in New York and break the deadlock. But in theatrical gesture of brinksmanship, he surprised the world by jumping back on a plane to Buenos Aires, thus snubbing his nose at the holdout creditors. In a statement issued to the financial press, Elliott wrote that "the Argentine government appears determined to default. We hope it chooses to avoid this dead-end path."

As the settlement talks in New York dragged on – and the deadline extended until July 30th – Argentine began to suffer serious financial consequences. When the end of July arrived without a settlement, headlines began blasting around the world that Argentina was in default. In a single day, the Argentine stock market dropped 8% and its international currency reserves were dangerously draining. Inflation, already at 15% for the first half of 2014, continued to be a serious threat. Despite the claims from Argentine officials that is was "absurd" to say that Argentina was in default, the global markets were convinced that the country was headed in that direction, and quickly.

# CHAPTER SIX

In early August, Argentina filed a claim with the International Court of Justice in The Hague in the hopes that it would reverse the U.S. federal court's decision that put it into default at the end of July. While it was going through the motions, Argentina's prospects in The Hague look pretty dim. For one thing, the United States would have to accept the International Court's jurisdiction, which it has done in only a handful of cases in the last seventy years.

The only remaining hope for Argentina was to find some diplomatic solution to the crisis. As Luis Moreno Ocampo, a former chief prosecutor for the International Criminal Court, said in an interview with *The Wall Street Journal,* "Argentina is looking for a solution knowing there is no way to formally appeal Griesa's ruling, which it considers unjust," With the focus shifting away from the legal to the diplomatic and political front, a heated debate has emerged about the international system – or lack thereof – for settling sovereign debt defaults."

Argentina was not alone is facing default. Both Grenada and the Republic of Congo were now in default. Grenada was sued by Taiwan's export agency in 2013 over debts that became impossible to repay after devastating hurricanes in 2004 and 2005. And Congo was sued by U.S.

investors for $69 million -- $50 million of which was interest and penalties. When a New York district court ruled against the Congo, the government appealed, arguing that African governments were at a disadvantage because of limited government capacity and poor legal representation in drafting the bond contracts.

On the face of it, there are reasonable arguments on both sides. Paul Singer and his defenders argue that Argentina has a legally enforceable debt and they must pay. Furthermore, it would be unfair for Argentina to pay those creditors who had reached a settlement and not pay the creditors who refused to settle. Singer's appeal is to common sense – they borrowed the money, now they should pay it back.

On the other side, Argentina and other critics of Judge Griesa's decision point out that there should be some mechanism for countries to settle their debts without being forced into default, which would harm not only the citizens of the country, but the global monetary system itself. Using the example of the American bankruptcy laws, they argue that an individual who is unable to pay can declare bankruptcy and have his debts reorganized in an orderly way. Why should countries be treated differently – condemned to what is a modern-day sovereign debtors prison?

There are passionate and articulate advocates on both sides of the debate. Jonathan Macy of the Yale School of Management wrote in *The New York Times*, "It is fair to require Argentina to choose between default and paying some of its creditors in full. The very definition of default is the failure of a party to fulfill its obligations under a valid contract. Not all contracts are fair, but absent fraud, contracts between parties who are capable of understanding the obligations they are entering into clearly are fair."

On the other side of the argument, there are those who argue it is unfair to penalize an entire nation for the mistakes of its leadership, who often are not even elected by the people. Ellen Appelbaum of the Center for Economic and Policy Research wrote "It's not fair to the government of Argentina, which cannot pay the vulture funds without facing demands from other creditors to be paid in full, a move which would open the country up to many billions of dollars of claims that it cannot possibly pay. Lastly, it is not fair to the tens and possibly hundreds of millions of people in countries who will face sovereign debt crises in the future."

Perhaps the most pointed debate is not over the fate of individual nations, but over the entire international system for settling sovereign debt. Nobel Prize-winning economist Joseph Stiglitz, writing in *The New York Times*, was harshly critical not only of the vulture funds, but also of the international system. "The vulture funds — the small number of creditors who held out from Argentina's earlier debt restructuring -- had no interest in the country or its people," wrote Stiglitz. "They picked up their bonds on the cheap, in hopes that by spending enough on litigation, they would eventually find a sympathetic judge who did not understand what was at issue and rule in their favor. All investors in sovereign bonds know that there is a risk of default — that's why the bonds can pay a far higher interest rate than U.S. bonds. But anyone buying bonds after a country announces a debt restructuring knows with virtual certainty that they will not be repaid in full without manipulating the legal system."

While there has been considerable concern voiced that Judge Griesa's ruling will disrupt the international monetary system, some observers believe that concern is overstated. Gabriel Sterne, head of global macro investor services at Oxford Economics and a former IMF economist, believes that Argentina is a special case. "Argentina is an anomaly," writes Sterne. "It would be wrong to think that Argentina has too much implication for sovereign debt and sovereign debt crises."

Stiglitz wrote that while the vulture funds have argued that they are pursuing the rule of law, they are actually undermining the rule of law by ignoring established precedents. Stiglitz cited an IMF proposal for a global system of debt settlement, which was endorsed by the United Nations, but later vetoed by the United States. The U.S. court, he adds, have made things much worse. "By transferring money from Argentina — where the per capita income is around $14,800 — to some billionaires will just create more inequality," writes Stiglitz. "But this is not just a question of fairness. The vultures have imposed enormous harm on global sovereign debt markets and on those countries whose well-being depends on them, especially in the emerging markets and developing countries."

While the debate raged over the impact of the Griesa decision in international financial and academic circles, the real-world impact was already being felt.  Debtor nations began to panic over an uncertain future, and creditors weighed their options for collecting on the debts. At the same time, international financial organizations were contemplating what to do in a post-Griesa world.   Did the global financial system need to pass a series of regulations now that the traditional "gentleman's agreement" form of debt restructuring had been summarily overturned?  Or would international credit markets become a chaotic version of the "Wild West?"

# CHAPTER SEVEN

With most legal remedies exhausted in the wake of the Griesa ruling, the battle between Paul Singer and Cristina Kirchner moved into the political arena. The day after Judge Griesa's fateful decision, Kirchner addressed the Argentine people in a nationally televised broadcast. "This opinion is contrary not only to Argentina's interests, but also to the 92% of the creditors who believed in the country and its debt restructuring, and it also goes against the functioning of the global economic and financial system," said Kirchner. "It is the validation of a business model on a global scale, a form of world domination based on speculation, for those businesses with securities and derivatives, to bring countries and their inhabitants to their knees. All they need are governments willing to cede to the pressures of this financial power."

After announcing her decision to fight the Griesa ruling, Kirchner introduced a bill in the Argentine Congress to make Buenos Aires rather than New York the place of payment for creditors and, in this way, get around the judge's ruling. However, Judge Griesa ruled that the potential legislation was illegal and could not be used to circumvent his ruling. In addition, growing opposition to the draft legislation in Argentine Congress meant that the likelihood for successful passage was diminishing.

Clearly, the debt crisis has become an explosive issue in Argentina's already explosive political culture. With Kirchner limited to two terms – her second term is up in 2015 – the political sharks are circling. Already two powerful candidates have emerged as her successor, both intent on distancing themselves from Kirchner's aggressive and stubborn stance against the bondholders, which many in Argentina associate with her more extreme Marxist views.

At the same time, Kirchner has sought to portray Argentina as the victim of the kind of predatory capitalism that is symbolized by Paul Singer's "vulture fund." She has used the strong nationalist streak in Argentina's culture to rally the population against the "imperialism" of Wall Street and unbridled capitalism. Protests have erupted around Argentina to protest U.S. economic policies and Argentina has taken out full-page ads in leading publications, including *The New York Times*, *The Wall Street Journal* and *The Financial Times* decrying the decision and its impact on not only Argentina, but developing nations around the world.

As Kirchner has fought back aggressively against the Griesa decision, Paul Singer has responded by taking up the cudgel against what he regards as Argentina's irresponsible position. The Singer-backed lobbying group American Task Force Argentina has led the attack and has launched the website factcheckargentina.org, which issues almost daily diatribes against Argentina's policies. In addition, advertisements have appeared in *The Wall Street Journal* and other major publications, attacking Argentina's failure to abide by the Griesa decision and make full payment on its debts.

Kirchner has appealed to the White House for some relief from the Griesa decision, arguing that President Obama could simply waive the ruling by declaring it an unconstitutional interference with his prerogative to conduct foreign policy. But it is unlikely that the White House will intervene. While the Obama administration has criticized the decision, since it seems unwilling to take the political risk of supporting a foreign government over an American creditor group, especially one led by a powerful Republican donor like Paul Singer.

Meanwhile, the international financial community has moved quickly to prevent any future debacles like the Argentine debt crisis from occurring again. The International Capital Market Association, a group of banks and investors, quickly adopted new standards to restrict vulture funds and holdout investors from undermining debt restructuring. The new rules would require all bondholders to be bound to a deal approved by 75 percent or more of the creditors "The potential adverse fallout globally from the default and restructuring of Argentina's debt demonstrates the important of having a clear, unambiguous contract terms for sovereign bonds," said Leland Goss, ICMA's general counsel.

While many in the international community appears ready to move past the Argentine debt crisis, the titanic struggle between

Kirchner and Singer continues. A number of prominent economists and political figures in Argentina have counseled Kirchner to end the battle and repay the debt, including Domingo Cavallo, the architect of Argentina's first debt restructuring deal in 2001 and an internationally renowned economist. "Argentina should comply with Judge Griesa's decision," Cavallo said at a recent conference.

Cavallo has been highly critical of Kirchner's handling of the crisis, calling it a disaster. "She wants to blame what is happening now on the vultures," he said, arguing that the debt crisis is only part of the economic crisis that is gripping Argentina. Cavallo contends that if a new government were able to stabilize the economy, then billions of dollars of capital that has left the country will return. Under these improved economic conditions, the government should be able to pay off the vulture investors. However, Kirchner appears unlikely to follow this advice as she has staked her political career on defeating Singer and the other vultures.

So who will ultimately win in this epic struggle between the Vulture and the Queen? Probably neither one. Even if she manages to fight off Singer, Queen Cristina is likely suffer an even deeper drop in popular support from the Argentine people. Once hailed as the "new Evita," Kirchner will be remembered primarily as the President who mishandled the debt crisis and brought the Argentine economy to the brink.

Paul Singer, the Vulture, is not likely to fair much better. While he may collect the bulk of the Argentine debts that he has struggled for decades to collect, he has paid an even higher price. His reputation as the "inventor of vulture funds" and the greedy investor who brought Argentina – along with several other developing countries to their knees – is firmly fixed. Among other things, this incident may make him poison in the political world, where he has enjoyed great influence in the past.

Perhaps more importantly for Singer, his lifelong strategy of buying sovereign debt at bargain basement prices and then collecting through aggressive litigation may also be in shambles. With the adoption of new rules governing sovereign debt by international finance organizations, the loopholes that Singer has long exploited will be permanently closed. And those institutions holding sovereign debt – banks and other financial organizations – will be much more reluctant to sell that debt to Singer and other vulture funds that have now officially become outlaws in the international financial system. Whether Singer's investors, who have profited from the vulture strategy in the past, will stick with him in the future is an open question.

Despite the fact that both the Vulture and the Queen are losers in the battle over Argentina's debt, there is no reason to weep for Paul Singer or Cristina Kirchner. Singer is likely to add millions to his already bulging bank account and Kirchner will likely serve out the rest of her term, and then retire to a comfortable life of luxury with the considerable nest egg that she and her husband managed to accumulate during their terms of office.

However, millions of Argentinians, along with millions of other people in developing countries around the world, will not be so lucky. Everything from the price of groceries to retiree's pensions will be impacted by the conflict between the Vulture and the Queen. Inflation has already seized Argentina, and unemployment is on the rise. Without access to international credit markets, the future looks bleak. For decades to come, Argentina will likely suffer from the default.

As for the rest of the world, it is not only poor countries like Congo and Grenada, but also European nations like Greece and Spain. The list of potential targets for vulture funds is endless, including a number of Eastern European, Asian, African and Latin American countries, from Ukraine to Mynamar. The question remains: Can the world stand by as future Vultures and Queens battle over a nation's future while its people can only watch helplessly?

# SOURCES

Abelson, Max and Porzecanski, Katia, "Paul Singer Will Make Argentina Pay" Business Week, August 7, 2014

Allen, Katie, "UN urged to swoop on vulture funds" theguardian.com, September 2, 2014

Barnato, Katy, "Not just Argentina: Other nations in debt doldrums" CNBC.com, September 2, 2014

Dayen, David, "Why Argentina's Crazy Debt Gambit Could Make Sense" The Fiscal Times, August 22, 2014

De Miguel, Veronique, "Argentina's Cristina Fernandez Kirchner: Woman, wife, first lady and president" VOXXI, July 19, 2012

De Sola, David "U.S. analysts sought details on mental health of Argentine president" CNN, December 1, 2010

Fernholz, Tim "The "vulture funds" are tired of being portrayed as the bad guys in Argentina's debt crisis" Quartz, August 19, 2014

Goni, Uki "Cristina Kirchner: she's not just another Evita" The Guardian, February 4, 2012

Goodman, Leah McGrath, "Axel Kicillof Is Argentina's Secret Weapon Against Default" Newsweek, July 30, 2014

Hong, Nicole, and Day, Matt, "U.S. Judge Says Argentina's Debt Swap Proposal Is Illegal" Wall Street Journal, August 21, 2014

Karabell, Zachary, "Argentina's financial woes can be partly blamed on one New York hedge fund" Slate.com August 1, 2014

Keenan, Terry, "Argentina president uses 'villian' Paul Singer" New York Post, August 31, 2014

Levine, Matt, "How Should Future Argentinas Treat Future Vultures?" Bloomberg View, August 29, 2014

Lopez, Linette, "Paul Singer Doesn't Understand Why We're So Obsessed With His Little Argentina Investment" Business Insider, July 30, 2014

Lopez, Linette, "Paul Singer's Next Trick Could Make The Argentine Government Way Angrier Than The Time He Took Its Boat" Business Insider, August 15, 2014

Lopez, Linette, "The Judge In The Argentina Vs. Hedge Funds Case Just Exposed A Big Weakness" Business Insider, August 22, 2014

Mount, Ian, El Calfate and Sherwell, Philip, "The Argentine president and her empire in the south" The Telegraph February 2012

Oakford, Samuel, "Vultures Circle as Argentina's Debt Crisis Gets Weird" VICE News July 1, 2014

Olive, David "Argentina has become the next global plaything" Toronto Star, August 25, 2014

Palast, Greg "How Barack Obama could end the Argentina debt crisis" The Guardian, August 7, 2014

Parks, Ken, "Argentina Economy Minister Axel Kicillof to Lead Debt Negotiating Team" Wall Street Journal, July 6, 2014

Perez, Santiago and Turner, Taos, "In Argentina, Mix of Money and Politics Stirs Intrigue Around Kirchner" Wall Street Journal July 28, 2014

Phelan, Stephen, "Argentina in latest debt default crisis pits 'motherland' against 'vultures'" The Guardian, August 20, 2014

Porzecanski, Katia "Washington Trip Provokes Call for Debt Talks: Argentina Credit" Bloomberg, July 3, 2014

Porzecanski, Katia and Russo, Camila, "George Soros has suddenly emerged as a key player in the fight over Argentina's debt" Bloomberg News, August 26, 2014

Reilly, Jill, "Fury in poverty-stricken Argentina as Cristina Kirchner is accused of spending £20,000 a day having newspapers delivered to her by Presidential jet" Daily Mail, July 30, 2014

Romero, Simon and Gilbert, Jonathan, "The Influential Minister Behind Argentina's Economic Shift" New York Times, January 26, 2014

Turner, Taos and Perez, Santiago, "Hedge Fund Targets Nevada Firms in Argentine Debt Dispute" Wall Street Journal, August 15, 2014

Ugeux, Georges, "The Obscene Escalation of the Vulture Funds Against Argentina" Huffington Post, August 17, 2014

Weiner, Bryan, "Leader Profiles: Cristina Kirchner" Center for Conflict Studies  Dec- 2013-Jan 2014

Wirz, Matt, "Hedge Funds File U.K. Suit Against BNY Mellon on Argentine Debt" Wall Street Journal, August 25, 2014